## WINNING THE BATTLE OF TEMPTATION

**The Invisible War—A Seven-Session Video-Based Study for Groups or Individuals**

PASTORRICK.COM

Published by Purpose Driven Publishers
23182 Arroyo Vista
Rancho Santa Margarita, CA 92688



ISBN: 978-1-4228-0314-1
Printed in the United States of America.

PX209501-20200406

# TABLE OF CONTENTS

**Session 1**
Understanding the Sources and Purposes of Temptation ........... 5

**Session 2**
The Process of Temptation ........ 13

**Session 3**
The Three Kinds of Temptation ........ 19

**Session 4**
God's Antidotes to Temptation ........ 27

**Session 5**
The Steps to Overcoming Temptation (Part One) ........ 33

**Session 6**
The Steps to Overcoming Temptation (Part Two) ........ 39

**Session 7**
How to Avoid Temptation ........ 45

# SESSION 1

## Understanding the Sources and Purposes of Temptation

# SESSION ONE

## Understanding the Sources and Purposes of Temptation

### TWO KINDS OF TESTING

**Trial:** A situation designed by God in order to ____________

______________________________ to him.

**Temptation:** A situation designed by Satan in order to ___

_______________________________________ from God.

*Consider it pure joy, my brothers, whenever you face trials of many kinds, because you know that the testing of your faith develops perseverance. Perseverance must finish its work so that you may be mature and complete, not lacking anything.*

James 1:2-4 (NIV)

*When tempted, no one should say, "God is tempting me." For God cannot be tempted by evil, nor does he tempt anyone.*

James 1:13 (NIV)

### GENERAL FACTS ABOUT TEMPTATION

It is not a _____________________________ to be tempted.

*Jesus was in all points tempted like as we are, yet he sinned not.*

Hebrews 4:15 (NKJV)

*Walk in the Spirit, and you shall not fulfill the lust of the flesh.*

Galatians 5:16 (NKJV)

I will never ________________________ temptation.

*No temptation has seized you except what is common to man. And God is faithful; he will not let you be tempted beyond what you can bear. But when you are tempted, he will also provide a way of escape so that you can stand up under it.*

1 Corinthians 10:13 (NIV)

Temptation will ____________________________________.

Temptations are ________________________ to everybody.

God __________________________ every temptation we go through.

God will _____________________________ if I trust him.

## THE THREE SOURCES OF TEMPTATION

- Your own ______________________________
- The ___________________________________
- The___________________________________

*When tempted, no one should say, "God is tempting me." For God cannot be tempted by evil, nor does he tempt anyone; but each person is tempted when, they are dragged away by their own evil desire and enticed. Then, after desire has conceived, it gives birth to sin; and sin, when it is fullgrown, gives birth to death.*

James 1:13-15 (NIV)

Lust is an unrighteous way to fulfill a

______________________________

*For everything in the world—the lust of the flesh, the lust of his eyes and the pride of life—comes not from the Father but from the world. The world and its desires pass away, but whoever does the will of God lives forever.*

1 John 2:16-17 (NIV)

The devil's purpose in temptation is to

______________________________

## WHY GOD ALLOWS TEMPTATION

The necessity of ______________________________

Temptation shows us:

- What we ______________________________
- Where we ______________________________
- Where we're ______________________________ in the future if we don't change.
- It allows a choice that is essential for character building. It's an opportunity for growth.

## DISCUSSION QUESTIONS

1. What did you hear?

   a. Was there a particular point that stuck out to you?

   b. Was there a Bible verse that spoke to you personally?

2. What do you think about what you heard?

3.What will you do? How will you put into practice what you heard?

# SESSION 2

## The Process of Temptation

# SESSION TWO

## The Process of Temptation

| | Step 1 | Step 2 | Step 3 |
|---|---|---|---|
| **The Process** | ____________ | ____________ | ____________ |
| **Satan's 3 Steps** | Satan ____________ God's Word | Satan gives his ____________ (John 8:44) | Satan offers an ____________ |
| **The Temptation of Adam (Genesis 3)** | *"Did God say?"* (vs. 1) | *"You shall not die."* (vs. 4) | *"Be wise now!"* (vs. 5) |
| **The Temptation of Jesus (Matthew 4:6)** | *"If you are the Son of God."* | Misquoted verse out of context (Psalm 91:11) | *"Be worshiped now!"* |
| **God's Truth** | *"Heaven and earth will pass away, but my words will never pass away."* (Mark 13:31) | *"You may be sure your sin will find you out."* (Numbers 32:23) | *"There is a way that seems right to a man, but in the end it leads to death."* (Proverbs 14:12) |
| **Correct response** | "Yes, he has said." Affirm God's Word. | Quote Scripture! | Wait for God's best. |

## LESSONS FROM MATTHEW 4:

• Just because you are filled with the Spirit doesn't mean you won't be tempted.

• Times of spiritual high are followed by temptation. After every mountain top, there is a valley.

• Satan often tempts us when our resistance is low.

• We are tempted, not just in our areas of weakness, but also in our areas of strength.

## DISCUSSION QUESTIONS

1. What did you hear?

   a. Was there a particular point that stuck out to you?

   b. Was there a Bible verse that spoke to you personally?

2. What do you think about what you heard?

3. What will you do? How will you put into practice what you heard?

# SESSION 3

## The Three Kinds of Temptation

# SESSION THREE

## The Three Kinds of Temptation

| | **Type 1** | **Type 2** | **Type 3** |
|---|---|---|---|
| **(1 John 2:16)** | Lust of the Flesh | Lust of the Eyes<br>(Proverbs 27:20) | Pride of Life |
| | Temptation to<br>____________<br>Desire to<br>____________ | Temptation to<br>____________<br>Desire to<br>____________ | Temptation to<br>____________<br>Desire to<br>____________ |
| | P ____________<br>Sex / Appetite | P ____________<br>Security / Avarice | P ____________<br>Success / Ambition |
| **Temptation of Adam & Eve (Genesis 3:6)** | *"The tree was good for ____________"* | *"It was pleasant to the ____________"* | *"You shall be as ____________"* |
| **Temptation of Jesus (Matthew 4)** | *"Turn these stones into bread."*<br>(vs. 3) | *"All these things will I give you."*<br>(vs. 9) | *"Jump off the pinnacle"*<br>(vs. 6) |
| **The Fall of Satan (Isaiah 14:12-16)** | *"I will ____________ to heaven."*<br>(to do)<br>(vs. 13) | *"I will ____________ my throne."*<br>(to have)<br>(vs. 13) | *"I will ____________ the most high."*<br>(to be)<br>(vs. 14) |
| **Moses (Hebrews 11:24-26)** | The World's Pleasure<br>(vs. 25) | The World's Treasure<br>(vs. 26) | The World's Measure<br>(vs. 24) |

*For we are not ignorant of how Satan works.*

2 Corinthians 2:11 (NIV)

*For everything that is in the world—the lust of the flesh, the lust of the eyes, and the pride of life does not come from the Father, but from the world. The world and its desires will pass away, but the man who does the will of God lives forever.*

1 John 2:16-1 (NIV)

*Now the serpent was more crafty than any of the wild animals the LORD God had made. He said to the woman, "Did God really say, 'You must not eat from any tree in the garden'?"*

*The woman said to the serpent, "We may eat fruit from the trees in the garden, but God did say, 'You must not eat fruit from the tree that is in the middle of the garden, and you must not touch it, or you will die.'"*

*"You will not surely die," the serpent said to the woman. "For God knows that when you eat of it your eyes will be opened, and you will be like God, knowing good and evil."*

*When the woman saw that the fruit of the tree was good for food and pleasing to the eye, and also desirable for gaining wisdom, she took some and ate it. She also gave some to her husband, who was with her, and he ate it. Then the eyes of both of them were opened, and they realized they were naked; so they sewed fig leaves together and made coverings for themselves.*

*Then the man and his wife heard the sound of the LORD God as he*

*was walking in the garden in the cool of the day, and they hid from the LORD God among the trees of the garden. But the LORD God called to the man, "Where are you?"*

*He answered, "I heard you in the garden, and I was afraid because I was naked; so I hid."*

*And he said, "Who told you that you were naked? Have you eaten from the tree that I commanded you not to eat from?"*

*The man said, "The woman you put here with me—she gave me some fruit from the tree, and I ate it."*

*Then the LORD God said to the woman, "What is this you have done?" The woman said, "The serpent deceived me, and I ate."*

Genesis 3:1-13 (NIV)

*Then Jesus was led by the Spirit into the desert to be tempted by the devil. After fasting forty days and forty nights, he was hungry. The tempter came to him and said, "If you are the Son of God, tell these stones to become bread."*

*Jesus answered, "It is written: 'Man does not live on bread alone, but on every word that comes from the mouth of God.'"*

*Then the devil took him to the holy city and had him stand on the highest point of the temple. "If you are the Son of God," he said,*

*"throw yourself down. For it is written: "'He will command his angels concerning you, and they will lift you up in their hands, so that you will not strike your foot against a stone.'"*

*Jesus answered him, "It is also written: 'Do not put the Lord your God to the test.'"*

*Again, the devil took him to a very high mountain and showed him all the kingdoms of the world and their splendor." All this I will give you," he said, "if you will bow dawn and worship me."*

*Jesus said to him, "Away from me, Satan! For it is written: 'Worship the Lord your God, and serve him only.'"*

Matthew 4:1-10 (NIV)

*How you have fallen from heaven, morning star, son of the dawn! You have been cast down to the earth, you who once laid low the nations! You said in your heart, "I will ascend to heaven; I will raise my throne above the stars of God; I will sit enthroned on the mount of assembly, on the utmost heights of the sacred mountain. 1 will ascend above the tops of the clouds; I will make myself like the Most High." But you are brought down to the grave, to the depths of the pit. Those who see you stare at you, they ponder your fate.*

Isaiah 14:12-16 (NIV)

*By faith Moses, when he had grown up, refused to be known as the son of Pharaoh's daughter. He chose to be mistreated along with the people of God rather than to enjoy the pleasures of sin for a short time. He regarded disgrace for the sake of Christ as of greater value than the treasures of Egypt, because he was looking ahead to his reward.*

Hebrews 11:24-26 (NIV)

## DISCUSSION QUESTIONS

1. What did you hear?

a. Was there a particular point that stuck out to you?

b. Was there a Bible verse that spoke to you personally?

2. What do you think about what you heard?

3. What will you do? How will you put into practice what you heard?

# SESSION 4

## God's Antidotes to Temptation

# SESSION FOUR

## God's Antidotes to Temptation

| | Type 1 | Type 2 | Type 3 |
|---|---|---|---|
| **(1 John 2:16)** | Lust of the Flesh | Lust of the Eyes (Proverbs 27:20) | Pride of Life |
| | Temptation to do<br>Desire to indulge | Temptation to have<br>Desire to increase | Temptation to be<br>Desire to impress |
| | Passion<br>Sex / Appetite | Possession<br>Security / Avarice | Position<br>Success / Ambition |
| **Worldly Philosophy** | Hedonism | Materialism | Secular Humanism |
| **Cultural Expressions** | "If it feels good, do it." | "Get all you can!" | "Look out for #1." |
| **The Challenge to God** | Challenges the ________ of God | Challenges the ________ of God | Challenges the ________ of God |
| **God's Antidotes (1 Corinthians 13:13)** | ________ always gives. | ________ stores up for Heaven. | ________ depends on God. |
| **Jesus' Answer (Matthew 16:24)** | ________ yourself. | ________ me.<br>Keep eyes on Jesus instead of things. | Take up your ________<br>No arrogance |

*And now these three remain: faith, hope and love. But the greatest of these is love.*

1 Corinthians 13:13 (NIV)

*Then Jesus said to his disciples, "If anyone would come after me, he must deny himself and take up his cross and follow me. For whoever wants to save his life will lose it, but whoever loses his life for me will find it. What good will it be for a man if he gains the whole world, yet forfeits his soul? Or what can a man give in exchange for his soul?"*

Matthew 16:24-26 (NIV84)

## DISCUSSION QUESTIONS

1. What did you hear?

   a. Was there a particular point that stuck out to you?

   b. Was there a Bible verse that spoke to you personally?

2. What do you think about what you heard?

3. What will you do? How will you put into practice what you heard?

# SESSION 5

## The Steps to Overcoming Temptation (Part One)

# SESSION FIVE

## The Steps to Overcoming Temptation (Part One)

*And lead us not into temptation, but deliver us from evil.*

Matthew 6:13 (KJV)

1. Identify what makes me ____________________

*Watch and pray so that you will not fall into temptation. The spirit is willing, but the flesh is weak.*

Matthew 26:41 (NIV)

- ______________ am I most tempted?
- ______________ am I most tempted?
- ______________ is with me when I'm most tempted?
- ______________ temporary benefit do I get if I give in?
- ______________ do I feel right before I'm tempted?

2. Plan to ____________________

*Plan carefully what you do... Avoid evil and walk straight ahead. Don't go one step off the right way."*

Proverbs 4:26-27 (GNT)

3. Guard my ____________________

*We are tempted by our own desires that drag us off and trap us.*

James 1:14 (CEV)

*"For from within, out of a person's heart, come evil thoughts, sexual immorality, theft, murder, adultery, greed, wickedness, deceit, lustful desires, envy, slander, pride, and foolishness."*

Mark 7:21-22 (NLT)

*Above all else, guard your heart, for it affects everything you do.*

Proverbs 4:23 (NLT96)

| | | |
|---|---|---|
| Physically exhausted | 0 1 2 3 4 | Energetic & in shape |
| Discouraged or pessimistic | 0 1 2 3 4 | Encouraged & hopeful |
| Bored & discontented | 0 1 2 3 4 | Challenged & contented |
| Spiritually dry or empty | 0 1 2 3 4 | Spiritually alive & growing |
| Alone or distant from others | 0 1 2 3 4 | Close to those you love |
| Insecure or unsure | 0 1 2 3 4 | Confident & secure |
| Wounded or deeply hurt | 0 1 2 3 4 | Loved & understood |
| Bitter or angry | 0 1 2 3 4 | Forgiven everyone |
| Sad | 0 1 2 3 4 | Happy |
| Feel like you've failed | 0 1 2 3 4 | Successful |

TOTAL: ________

*Do not give the devil a foothold.*

Ephesians 4:27 (NIV)

## DISCUSSION QUESTIONS

1. What did you hear?

   a. Was there a particular point that stuck out to you?

   b. Was there a Bible verse that spoke to you personally?

2. What do you think about what you heard?

3. What will you do? How will you put into practice what you heard?

# SESSION 6

## The Steps to Overcoming Temptation (Part Two)

# SESSION SIX

## The Steps to Overcoming Temptation (Part Two)

4. Pray for ____________________________

*Call on me in [your] day of trouble; I will deliver you, and you will honor me.*
Psalm 50:15 (NIV)

*[Jesus] understands our weaknesses, for he faced all of the same temptations we do, yet he did not sin. So let us come boldly to . . . our gracious God. There we will receive his mercy, and . . . grace to help us when we need it."*
Hebrews 4:15-16 (NLT96)

5. Turn my ____________________________ elsewhere

*Thinking about your commands will keep me from doing some foolish thing.*
Psalm 119:6 (CEV)

*Each one is tempted when, by his own evil desire, he is dragged away and enticed. Then, aft er desire has conceived, it gives birth to sin; and sin, when it is full-grown, gives birth to death.*
James 1:14-15 (NIV84)

## THE PREDICTABLE PATTERN OF TEMPTATION

- ____________________________________
- ____________________________________
- ____________________________________

*Don't let evil conquer you, but conquer evil with good.*

Romans 12:21 (GW)

6. Get a ______________________ or a ______________________

*Two are better than one, because together . . . if one falls down, the other can help him up. But if someone is alone and falls . . . there is no one to help him.*

Ecclesiastes 4:9-10 (GNT)

*Brothers and sisters, if someone in your group does something wrong, you who are spiritual should go to that person and gently help make him right again. But be careful, because you might be tempted to sin, too. By helping each other with your troubles, you truly obey the law of Christ.*

Galatians 6:1-2 (NCV)

## THREE BENEFITS OF SHARING YOUR TEMPTATION WITH OTHERS:

- It's ______________________
- It's ______________________
- It's ______________________

*My dear friends, if you know people who have wandered off from God's truth, don't write them off. Go after them. Get them back and you will have rescued precious lives!*

James 5:19-20 (The Message)

## DISCUSSION QUESTIONS

1. What did you hear?

    a. Was there a particular point that stuck out to you?

    b. Was there a Bible verse that spoke to you personally?

2. What do you think about what you heard?

3. What will you do? How will you put into practice what you heard?

# SESSION 7

## How to Avoid Temptation

# SESSION SEVEN

## How to Avoid Temptation

*Watch and pray that [you] enter not into temptation.*

Matthew 26:41 (KJV)

*Let him who thinks he stands take heed lest he fall.*

1 Corinthians 10:12 (NKJV)

*Be careful how you walk, not as unwise men, but as wise.*

Ephesians 5:15 (NASB)

*Be on the alert, stand firm in the faith, act like men, be strong.*

1 Corinthians 16:13 (NASB)

## PRACTICAL STEPS TO AVOID TEMPTATION

1. Make sure your ____________________ have been dealt with.

*Timothy, my son, I give you this instruction in keeping with the prophecies once made about you, so that by following them you may fight the good fight, holding on to faith and a good conscience. Some have rejected these and so have shipwrecked their faith.*

1 Timothy 1:18-19 (NIV84)

2. Make sure you are filled daily with the ____________________

*Walk in the Spirit, and you shall not fulfill the lust of the flesh.*

Galatians 5:16 (NKJV)

3. Decide in advance to ____________________________

4. Put on ____________________________________

*Therefore put on the full armor of God, so that when the day of evil comes, you may be able to stand your ground, and after you have done everything, to stand. Stand firm then, with the belt of truth buckled around your waist, with the breastplate of righteousness in place, and with your feet fitted with the readiness that comes from the gospel of peace. In addition to all this, take up the shield of faith, with which you can extinguish all the flaming arrows of the evil one. Take the helmet of salvation and the sword of the Spirit, which is the word of God.*

Ephesians 6:13-17 (NIV)

5. Minimize the ______________________________ and maximize the

____________________________ of giving in.

## SIX CONSEQUENCES OF UNCONFESSED SIN

• Fellowship with God is _____________________________

*Restore to me the JOY of your salvation.*

Psalm 51:12 (NIV)

*If we claim to have fellowship with him yet walk in the darkness, we lie and do not live the truth. But if we walk in the light, as he is in the light, we have fellowship with one another, and the blood of Jesus, his Son, purifies us from all sin. If we claim to be without sin, we deceive ourselves and the truth is not in us. If we confess our sins, he is faithful and just and will forgive us our sins and purify us from all unrighteousness. If we claim we have not sinned, we make him out to be a liar and his word has no place in our lives.*

1 John 1:6-10 (NIV84)

• My prayers will not be _____________________________

*But your iniquities have separated you from your God; your sins have hidden his face from you, so that he will not hear.*

Isaiah 59:2 (NIV)

*If anyone turns a deaf ear to my instruction, even their prayers are detestable.*

Proverbs 28:9 (NIV)

*Whoever conceals their sins does not prosper, but the one who confesses and renounces them finds mercy.*

Proverbs 28:13 (NIV)

*Then they will cry out to the LORD, but he will not answer them. At that time he will hide his face from them because of the evil they have done.*

Micah 3:4 (NIV)

*If I had not confessed the sin in my heart, the Lord would not have listened.*

Psalm 66:18 (NLT)

*Husbands, in the same way be considerate as you live with your wives, and treat them with respect as the weaker partner and as heirs with you of the gracious gift of life, so that nothing will hinder your prayers.*

1 Peter 3:7 (NIV)

- God ______________________________ using me.

*Who may ascend into the hill of the Lord? Or who may stand in His holy place? He who has clean hands and a pure heart, who has not lifted up his soul to an idol, nor sworn deceitfully. He shall receive blessing from the Lord, and righteousness from the God of his salvation.*

Psalm 24:3-5 (NKJV)

*For the eyes of the Lord run to and fro throughout the whole earth, to shew himself strong in the behalf of them whose heart is perfect toward him.*

2 Chronicles 16:9 (KJV)

- God will ______________________________ me.

Punishment is retribution for the past. Discipline is correction for the future.

*Those whom l love I rebuke and discipline. So be earnest, and repent.*

Revelation 3:19 (NIV)

*As you endure this divine discipline, remember that God is treating you as his own children. Who ever heard of a child who is never disciplined by its father? If God doesn't discipline you as he does all of his children, it means that you are illegitimate and are not really his children at all. Since we respected our earthly fathers who disciplined us, shouldn't we submit even more to the discipline of the Father of our spirits, and live forever?*

Hebrews 12:7-9 (NLT)

• God cannot ______________________________ me.

*The man without the Spirit does not accept the things that come from the Spirit of God, for they are foolishness to him, and he cannot understand them, because they are spiritually discerned.*

1 Corinthians 2:14 (NIV84)

• I am vulnerable to Satan's ______________________________

6. Guard your ____________________________________

*So think clearly and exercise self-control. Look forward to the special blessings that will come to you at the return of Jesus Christ.*

1 Peter 1:13 (NLT96)

## DISCUSSION QUESTIONS

1. What did you hear?

   a. Was there a particular point that stuck out to you?

   b. Was there a Bible verse that spoke to you personally?

2. What do you think about what you heard?

3. What will you do? How will you put into practice what you heard?